Bethlehem's Closet — A Reunion Of Grace

Monologues, Children's Sermons,
And Worship Bulletins
For Advent And Christmas

Donald H. Neidigk

CSS Publishing Company, Inc., Lima, Ohio

BETHLEHEM'S CLOSET — A REUNION OF GRACE

Copyright © 2002 by
CSS Publishing Company, Inc.
Lima, Ohio

All rights reserved. The worship bulletins may be copied for use as intended. No other part of this publication may be reproduced in any manner whatsoever without the prior permission of the publisher, except in the case of brief quotations embodied in critical articles and reviews. Inquiries should be addressed to: Permissions, CSS Publishing Company, Inc., P.O. Box 4503, Lima, Ohio 45802-4503.

Scripture quotations are from the *Holy Bible, New International Version.* Copyright 1973, 1978, 1984 International Bible Society. Used by permission of Zondervan Bible Publishers. All rights reserved.

For more information about CSS Publishing Company resources, visit our website at www.csspub.com or e-mail us at custserv@csspub.com or call (800) 241-4056.

ISBN 0-7880-1909-0   PRINTED IN U.S.A.

*To my parents,
Oscar and Rhoda Neidigk*

Table Of Contents

Introduction	7
Advent 1	
Grandmother Tamar — A Wronged Widow	9
Children's Sermon	15
Worship Bulletin	17
Advent 2	
Grandmother Rahab — A Former Prostitute	21
Children's Sermon	27
Worship Bulletin	29
Advent 3	
Grandmother Ruth — A Moabite Convert	33
Children's Sermon	40
Worship Bulletin	42
Christmas Eve	
Mary — A Young Mother	45
Children's Sermon	51
Worship Bulletin	53
Christmas Day	
Grandmother Bathsheba — A Violated Wife	59
Children's Sermon	65
Worship Bulletin	67

Introduction

An Advent series based on the genealogy of Jesus? Pastor, what could be more boring? Not only that, but an Advent series that considers the lives of women such as Tamar, Rahab, Ruth, and Bathsheba, women referred to by Matthew as grandmothers of Jesus? Pastor, what are you thinking? There are some very embarrassing events in the lives of those women! Couldn't we just do shepherds and wise men as usual?

Yes, I know it's a bit out of the ordinary. And I admit that on the surface, genealogies can seem boring. Many are the people who have set out to read the Bible through from cover to cover only to get bogged down and quit when they encounter the genealogies in Genesis, or perhaps those in the Gospels of Matthew or Luke. I'd have to agree, one should never try reading through a genealogy on a warm summer afternoon with a full stomach. You'll be taking a nap before you know it.

But genealogies are included for a reason. and so are the sordid stories behind some of the names, as offensive as those stories might be. In his wisdom, God decided that we should be aware of these people and events, and thus he inspired the Bible writers to put pen to paper and tell us about them.

But why? What possible reason could God have for wanting us to know about the strange and sometimes immoral behavior of the ancestors of Jesus? Because these stories relate to our redemption, that's why. God wants us to realize that the family into which Jesus was born was just like your family and my family, a family with a past, an imperfect family in need of a Savior. Jesus is that Savior. But he's no ivory tower Savior, untouchable, so high above us he can't relate to our lives and problems. God could have instructed Moses and Matthew to clean up their stories, and present the Bible's characters in a more noble light, but he didn't. God could have caused their stories to be told in the way most of us learned about American heroes. They were always above corruption. George Washington, we were taught, never told a lie. And because of that, George Washington will forever be on a pedestal high above the rest of us.

But not Jesus. Jesus came from a family we can relate to, a family of sinners who often had tragic, troubled lives. He came from the same human muck as we, with just one difference, whereas we've sinned, he hasn't. Our temptations, our sorrows and disappointments, relatives whose stories are just as embarrassing as our own — all these Jesus shares with us. And that makes him a sympathetic Savior, exactly the kind we need.

Sometimes our sins and problems and weaknesses so humiliate us we want to hide; we want to move away to some place where no one knows us. But because of Jesus we don't have to. Jesus' family, with all their baggage, stayed in the same small geographical area. How could they do that? Because they were the forgiven people of God, people whose guilt would be laid on a Grandson to be born someday in Bethlehem.

He was born for us, too. Through Jesus our guilt is taken far away and we and our families have a fresh start everyday. Jesus came, Saint Paul says, "... when the time had fully come." When our situation was hopeless, "God sent his Son, born of a woman, born under law, to redeem those under law, that we might receive the full rights of sons" (Galatians 4:4). As a child of God, you can hold your head high, no matter what your past, or what's in your family's closet.

So this Advent Season, we join the family of Jesus for a Reunion of Grace at Bethlehem. Together we will sit around a table and hear the stories of several women who were redeemed just as we were, by Jesus, whose birth all of us celebrate. And now for our first story ...

Advent I Genesis 38:6-7, 11-19, 24-30
Matthew 1:1-3; Deuteronomy 25:5-10

Grandmother Tamar — A Wronged Widow

This is the party, isn't it? This is the reunion for the family of Jesus, right? Good! For a moment, I thought I must have had the wrong house, maybe even the wrong town. From the way you all were looking at me, I was beginning to think I wasn't welcome. But the invitation clearly states that all the ancestors of Jesus are invited. I'm Tamar, a great-grandmother of Jesus many times over, so I must be included.

Oh, you already know me? So that's why you're feeling so uncomfortable! You'd rather not have a twice-widowed woman, and a prostitute, and an adulteress as well, spoil your party. I suppose I could go on the offensive here and remind you of a few things from your background, but I won't. Since all of us are just sinners saved by God's grace, why don't we just let bygones be bygones? Shall we? Good!

I can see you're still feeling a bit awkward. Very well. Though I owe no one an explanation for what I did, I'd be happy to give you one. Perhaps knowing my side of the story might make you feel a little better. I'm not proud of my past, and I do take responsibility for my actions. But I don't know what else I could have done, the times being what they were. A woman had few rights in my world.

As a woman, my purpose in life was to bear children for my husband, especially sons. Sons meant that my husband's name would be carried on and whatever property he had accumulated would be kept in the family. Sons meant that I would be provided for in my old age. There were no pension plans, no Social Security. Marriage and children meant everything to a woman.

But I couldn't choose whom I would marry. That was entirely the decision of my father and future father-in-law. They arranged everything. Once an agreement had been reached and I was given to a man to be his wife, my future was settled, and for the most part, secure. I would belong to my husband's family. Should my husband die, his family would provide another husband for me. That way I could still be a mother and be taken care of when I grew old.

It was an ancient system, with roots in Mesopotamia, developed even long before Abraham. Moses, who came many years after me, put it down in writing. It was called the Law of Levirate Marriage. If my husband died, his brother was to marry me. The first child of that union would become the child of my deceased husband. Any inheritance would become that child's inheritance. It wouldn't pass on to my new husband. My new husband would assume any debts I'd been left with.

As you can see, marrying a husband's widow, as the law required, was full of pitfalls and responsibilities, pitfalls and responsibilities many men would rather not have. But with few rights, it was one of the few benefits a woman could count on. That is, it was a benefit a woman could count on if the men to whose family she belonged obeyed the law.

The men in my new family didn't. That's why I did the things I did, shameful though they might seem to you. It all began when my father arranged to have me marry Judah's son, Er. Even that was against the wishes of Yahweh, Judah's God. My family was Canaanite, and pagan. But Judah didn't seem to care. He'd already compromised so much in his relationship with Yahweh. First he'd married a Canaanite woman himself, opening the doors to idolatry in his family. Then, out of jealousy, he'd joined in the plot to have his brother Joseph sold into slavery. Perhaps guilt is why he moved away from his father.

At any rate, near his new home in the hill country west of Jerusalem, Judah and my father arranged to have me given to Er, Judah's oldest son. I'd never have chosen him, an immoral, irreligious man, wicked in the eyes of Yahweh. Though he was dishonest and cruel, I was a good wife to him in those few months we were married. But Yahweh was merciful. Soon after I came into Er's tent, he died, and I was freed from him. But not from Judah's family or the law. Since Er left me childless, Judah, in obedience to the centuries-old custom, gave me Er's brother, Onan.

It fell to Onan to become my husband and raise up a son on behalf of his brother Er. Both brothers were repugnant examples of manhood. But who cared what I thought? With Er gone, Onan became the eldest son of Judah, and stood to inherit the greatest portion of the estate. But if he fathered a child for his brother Er, Onan's slice of the inheritance pie would be much smaller. So he pretended to become my husband, casting his seed on the ground, instead of planting it in my womb. It was an evil, selfish thing he did. And Yahweh punished him with death.

There was still one son left to Judah, Shelah, just a boy when these things happened. As the law required, Judah promised Shelah to me as soon as he was of age. But Judah's promise meant nothing. He made it just to appear righteous, but he had no intention of keeping it.

Well, you know how it was in those days. Without a husband and children, I had no hope, no respect, no dignity, no future. Against Yahweh's laws, Judah sent me to live with my father. Years passed, and Shelah grew up. I was still a relatively young woman, but Judah turned a deaf ear to my needs and refused to acknowledge his responsibility. As a woman and a member of Judah's family, I was trapped. I was not allowed to marry outside of that family, yet the only man eligible was not given to me. I was humiliated and embarrassed. I was powerless to do anything about it. Or was I?

That's when my little scheme came to me. Judah's wife had died. I knew that after his grief had subsided, he would be lonely. He would want the company of a woman. I determined that I would be that woman. My opportunity came when Judah and his friend Hirah took the sheep to Timnath at shearing time. It was a joyful occasion, shearing time. In the spring dozens of herdsman would come together with their flocks. Skilled shearers would clip away the thick winter wool of the sheep. It was something like the fall harvest festivals. There was music and dancing. The wine flowed freely, there by the waters of the two springs of Enaim where everyone gathered. There I covered myself in the garments of a prostitute, waiting for Judah to come by. No one would suspect me as being Tamar, his daughter-in-law, blending in as I did with all the other revelers. Soon I saw him, there in the crowd, and he me.

"Let me sleep with you!" he said with the drunken confidence of a rich old man who had nothing to fear. With my face veiled coyly, he didn't recognize me.

"What will you give me if I let you come in to me?" I asked brazenly, standing as seductively as I could by the doorway of the small tent I had set up.

"I'll send you a young goat from my flock as soon as I get home."

"I'll need something as a pledge."

"But I have nothing with me."

"Give me your seal and staff," I demanded.

Overcome with lust, he gave in. That cylinder seal on a cord and the ornately carved staff would become my most precious possessions, indeed the only things that would stand between death and me.

The sordid act done, Judah faded back into the crowd. I quickly changed into my widow's garb, put the seal around my neck and with Judah's staff in hand, returned to the home of my father. Three months later, it became known that I, a widow of many years, was pregnant.

Meanwhile, Judah had also returned home. True to his promise, he had sent his friend Hirah with the young goat to find the prostitute and pay her. But he didn't find her. I wasn't there. And no one had seen anyone matching my description. Afraid he'd look like a fool, Judah called off the search. Meanwhile I guarded closely the two items that would disgrace him more than me.

News of an unwed woman becoming pregnant travels fast in every era, including mine. Judah was enraged when he heard of my indiscretion. As a female member of his family, he had the power of life and death over me. Adultery in my day was punishable by stoning. Often the corpse would be burned as a warning to anyone else who might behave so wickedly. That was Judah's plan for me.

I was dragged from my home to answer the charges. I suspect that Judah was secretly delighted that I had committed adultery.

He hadn't wanted to give his third son, Shelah, to me anyway. Stoning me was his way out of the obligation. Now Judah would be free to find a safer wife for his son.

But I was smarter than Judah. Just before the stones began to fly, I tore the seal from my neck and flung the staff on the ground before my accuser and the jury he had assembled. "I am pregnant by the man who owns these," I shouted out.

At once the hypocrisy of Judah became apparent. A public follower of the Law of Yahweh, yet privately, a sinner, Judah was forced to confess. "She is more righteous than I."

Yes, what I did was wrong, but it forced Judah to keep his obligation before Yahweh, to provide me a husband who would father my children. He would never willingly give me his surviving son, Shelah, the son whom he planned would inherit his estate and blessing. So I, by my scheming and the intervention of Yahweh, took matters into my own hands. Yes, I sinned, but God in his mercy turned my sin into a blessing. To me, a wronged widow, he gave two sons by Judah, twins Zerah and Perez.

Through me, God kept his promise to Abraham and Isaac and Jacob, of a descendant through whom all the world would be blessed. Through me, God fulfilled the prophecy Jacob gave on his deathbed, "The scepter shall not depart from Judah." It was through me, through my son Perez, that one day David, Israel's greatest king, would be born, and from his line, Jesus, the King of kings, whose birth we celebrate today at this reunion of grace in Bethlehem.

So now you know my story. Now you know why I, a twice-married widow, a prostitute, an adulteress, have the right to be among you. I claim no moral purity of my own, no righteousness or virtue. I, like you, am here today, as a poor handmaiden of God's grace. Yes, I've sinned much. But my own great-grandson, whose birth we all celebrate, has forgiven me, and made me worthy to be here.

Now, if you'll excuse me, I wonder if you'd make room for me at the table with you? There, that's better. But don't get too comfortable. There are more like me coming. As a matter of fact, I think I hear Rahab, the harlot, another great-grandmother of Jesus, coming up the path.

Prayer

Gracious Lord, Yahweh, God of Tamar, my God, I wonder at how you took the troubled past of this woman and used it to bring about your plan of redemption. Thank you for the Savior who descended from her, Jesus, in every way like me except for my sin. Thank you, Lord, that through Jesus, great-grandson of Tamar, I am forgiven of all my sins and welcomed at your reunion of grace. Amen.

Advent 1 — Children's Sermon

"And you also were included in Christ when you heard the word of truth, the Gospel of your salvation. Having believed, you were marked in him with a seal, the promised Holy Spirit."
— Ephesians 1:13

Items needed: A wax seal or the church's official seal

Good evening, boys and girls. Welcome to our first Advent service. In the Old Testament lesson we read the sad story of Tamar who was about to be killed for doing something that was against God's law, that is, having a baby without being married. No one knew who the father of the baby was, so only the woman was going to be punished.

In those days, they would throw stones at the guilty person until he or she died. I'm glad we don't do that today, aren't you? In the story of Tamar, just at the last minute, before they started throwing the stones at her, Tamar pulled out a special seal and staff and said, "The man who owns these is the father." The man was Judah. He was the father and he was the one who was going to throw the rocks. I'm glad Tamar had kept Judah's seal and staff. They saved her life.

I brought a seal with me to show you what one looks like. *(Demonstrate how the seal works.)* In the old days, a seal was pressed into hot wax leaving a picture. Nowadays, most seals are mechanical. They press a picture or design onto a piece of paper. A seal is like a signature. It makes something official. Important church documents have the church seal on them.

In Bible times, a person's seal was his ID, like a driver's license is today. It proved who you were or guaranteed that what you said was true. When Tamar showed everyone Judah's seal, it proved she wasn't lying and kept the people from stoning her. The seal saved her life.

There's a seal that saves our lives too. It's a seal that says you are God's child; that you belong to him. Do you know what it is? *(Let children guess at the answer.)* The seal is Holy Baptism. We are guilty sinners who deserve death. But God has given us a seal that saves us, and that seal is Baptism. In our Baptism, God joins us to Jesus who died in our place to forgive our sins. In Baptism, God gives us his Holy Spirit to be with us and protect us from all our enemies forever.

I'm thankful for that seal, aren't you? Let's thank God for Holy Baptism, God's seal that protects us.

Prayer

Dear Father in heaven, I know I have sinned. I've done things you don't want me to do, and I deserve to be punished. But thank you for sending Jesus to be my Savior, to die for me and forgive me all my sins. Thank you that in my Baptism, the Holy Spirit comes to me and protects me from all my enemies. In Jesus' name I pray. Amen.

Worship Bulletin

Bethlehem's Closet — A Reunion Of Grace
Meditations For Advent From The Family of Jesus

We Approach Our Gracious God

Hymn "Savior Of The Nations, Come" (vv. 1-3)

Invocation
P: In the name of the Father and of the Son and of the Holy Spirit,
C: Amen.

Psalm 25 (Selected verses)
P: To you, O Lord, I lift up my soul; in you I trust, O my God.
C: Do not let me be put to shame, nor let my enemies triumph over me.
P: But they will be put to shame who are treacherous without excuse.
C: Remember not the sins of my youth, and my rebellious ways.
All: According to your love remember me, for you are good, O Lord.

Hymn "Savior Of The Nations, Come" (vv. 4-6)

We Hear God's Gracious Word

The First Lesson Genesis 38:6-7, 11-19, 24-30
"She is more righteous than I."

L: This is the record of the family of Jesus,
C: As was Tamar, I am a sinner in need of God's grace.

The Holy Gospel Matthew 1:1-3
"Judah [was] the father of Perez and Zerah whose mother was Tamar."

P: It was for the salvation of this family that Jesus was born.
C: **I am his family. He will save his people from their sins.**

Children's Sermon

Hymn "Lo, How A Rose"

Sermon "Grandmother Tamar — A Wronged Widow"

We Respond In Faith To God's Gracious Word

The Apostles' Creed
I believe in God the Father Almighty, maker of heaven and earth.
    And in Jesus Christ, his only Son, our Lord, who was conceived by the Holy Spirit, born of the virgin Mary, suffered under Pontius Pilate, was crucified, died and was buried. He descended into hell. The third day he rose again from the dead. He ascended into heaven, and sits at the right hand of God the Father Almighty. From thence he will come to judge the living and the dead.
    I believe in the Holy Spirit, the holy Christian Church, the communion of saints, the forgiveness of sins, the resurrection of the body, and the life everlasting. Amen.

Offering

Offering Voluntary

Prayer Of The Day (Unison)
Gracious Lord, Yahweh, God of Tamar, my God, I wonder at how you took the troubled past of this woman and used it to

bring about your plan of redemption. Thank you for the Savior who descended from her, Jesus, in every way like me except for my sin. Thank you, Lord, that through Jesus, great-grandson of Tamar, I am forgiven of all my sins and welcomed at your reunion of grace. Amen.

Pastoral Prayers

Response
P: Grandson of Tamar, Savior,
C: hear our prayer.

The Lord's Prayer (Unison)
Our Father, who art in heaven, hallowed be thy name, thy kingdom come, thy will be done on earth as it is in heaven.

Give us this day our daily bread; and forgive us our trespasses as we forgive those who trespass against us; and lead us not into temptation, but deliver us from evil.

For thine is the kingdom and the power and the glory forever and ever. Amen.

We Go Forth To Live God's Gracious Word

Concluding Sentences And Benediction
P: Jesus, Grandson of Tamar, is our Brother.
C: **Yes, Grandson of Tamar, our Brother, yet more than a brother, also the Son of God, our Savior.**
P: To him who is able to keep you from falling and to present you before his glorious presence without fault and with great joy — to the only God our Savior be glory, majesty, power, and authority, through Jesus Christ our Lord, before all ages, now and forevermore. Amen.

Closing Hymn "Let All Together Praise Our God"

(Note: Hymns in these services are suggested and may be changed to fit local circumstances.)

Advent 2   Joshua 2:1-24
Matthew 1:1-5a; Hebrews 11:29-31; James 2:25-26

Grandmother Rahab — A Former Prostitute

I thought this was the reunion for the family of Jesus? It is, you say? Then why so many men and so few women? Aside from Mary, the mother of Jesus, I see only Tamar. Oh, I remember. In my day, men were the most important members of the family. We women were only necessary to bear children and keep our husbands organized. Our unseen efforts allowed our husbands to assume the positions of prominence in the community, such as elder at the city gate.

I, like many other grandmothers of Jesus, would have gone unmentioned in his genealogy had I not been or done something very much out of the ordinary. Tamar, whom I see you've already met, and I were among those exceptional women. Unforgettable women and troublesome women, I might add. You might call us flies in the ointment.

Why are you looking at me that way? You're surprised at my appearance? What did you expect, a glamour girl, slender and alluring, with fashionable hair and make-up to match? Perhaps that's the Rahab of popular imagination, but it's not I. As my name implies, I'm just a fat, plain woman, broad as a barn door. Perhaps not very appealing to you, but many found me quite desirable in my younger days, including Salmon, the spy I eventually married.

Faithful Jews and Christians alike give me praise for hiding Salmon and that other spy; keeping secret their presence in Jericho so the king would not kill them. That deed everyone remembers. But to this day, many are still troubled by the fact that I was a prostitute and a liar. Such gymnastics believing people go through to protect my reputation! Thanks, but I don't need your efforts.

Some try to whitewash my past, claiming I wasn't really a prostitute at all, but rather a hostess, an innkeeper. Some might suggest that I was something more than a street woman, that I was in fact a shrine prostitute, a woman dedicated to the fertility goddess, and therefore someone who saw herself as a woman of faith and devotion, be it ever so misguided. Let me set the record straight. I was a harlot, nothing more. I was an unmarried woman who provided a seamy form of entertainment to the men of Jericho, and any traveler who might come along. Why else do you suppose I no longer lived at home with my father and mother, my brothers and sisters? They were ashamed of me, as any family would be.

Oh, I had other work. In my house built high into the wall of the city, I plied a very legitimate trade, making linen cloth from flax, weaving into it my own distinctive designs with scarlet yarn. But it was time-consuming work, work that didn't pay nearly as well as my other business. But even I, a Canaanite and a pagan, knew better. God's law had been written on my heart just as it has been on yours.

I would be untruthful though if I said my conscience was clear. It wasn't. And it troubled me even more as I heard the reports of Israel's victories over our neighbors. For decades we had been aware of how Israel had left Egypt; how Yahweh had parted the Red Sea for the refugees to pass, but closing it again over Pharaoh's army, drowning them all. We'd heard that Yahweh had promised Canaan to Israel to punish us for our idolatry and immorality. Talk about offensive! Who were the Israelites and their God to tell us we were wrong and to take our land because of it? Most of the nations of the world, including ours, worshiped many gods, and even sacrificed our children to them. We were as sincere in our beliefs as they were in theirs. The very idea of their arrogance!

Besides, for a while it seemed that their exodus from Egypt was merely an accident. Their first attempts at conquest of our land failed. Israel was reduced to wandering in the desert and foraging for whatever food they could find on the desert floor. They were no threat, that rag-tag tribe of gypsies. Habiru, we called them. Ours was an ancient culture. Our cities were walled and strong. Our armies well equipped and trained. We'd withstood many invasions. We'd withstand another.

For 38 years the Habiru were a laughing stock to the world, forsaken by their God, Yahweh, wandering aimlessly about in the desert, homeless. But then came disturbing news. Our allies to the east across the Jordan, the Amorite kingdoms of Sihon and Og, had fallen to them. We had relied on them to repulse the invading Habiru. Sihon and Og were descendants of the Babylonians, a nation that centuries before had ruled the world. Surely they could stop that pathetic rabble from the desert!

But they couldn't. The Amorite kingdoms were destroyed before the onslaught of shepherds and herdsmen armed with little more than the tools of a farmer. They had no armor, no bright uniforms, no chariots. They had only the name of their God, Yahweh, and his promise, and their enemies melted before them. The Amorite priests prayed to their gods. They offered sacrifice. Their seers prophesied victory. But the victory belonged to Israel.

I began to doubt my own gods and their ability to turn back Israel when the invasion we all knew was coming finally came. If Sihon and Og, powerful kings that they were, couldn't break the Israelite tide, who was the unimportant king of Jericho to attempt the task? At some point, I don't recall just when, I found myself convinced that my gods were no gods at all, that my king could not protect me, that if my family and I were to survive I would have to seek shelter under the wings of Yahweh. He alone was God.

Even more, I'd heard of the Law Yahweh had commanded his people to keep. When his people conquered mine, how could I expect to receive mercy when I knew I lived in shameless contempt of that Law? It was for the very idolatry and immorality that I had practiced that my nation was about to be destroyed and given to another. While the king, his army, and our whole city were feverishly planning for the coming siege, I was weighted down with a sense of guilt and despair. I knew that Jericho, strong as it might be, could never stand against Yahweh, the God of heaven and earth.

Hardly had this new faith begun incubating in my heart when the two spies of Israel knocked at my door. They came to my house because it would attract the least attention and because I, as a prostitute, might know a great deal. The customers of a prostitute include the likes of all sorts of men, the rich and powerful as well as the common laborer and soldier. And often those customers, with tongues loosened by wine, and eager to seem important, cast caution aside along with their garments, and divulge secrets they should share with no one, especially a prostitute.

The two spies were hoping I would know some of those secrets. They came with words of flattery about my beauty. I laughed. Even I knew that with my weight I was hardly beautiful. Next they tried gifts and bribes, hoping they could buy my secrets. Before I could explain that none of this was necessary, there was a pounding and shouting at my door. "Rahab, bring out the men who came to you. They're spies. Be quick or we'll break down the door!"

Frantically I pointed to the stairs, whispering hoarsely, "Hurry! Up there! The flax pile on the roof; get under it! I'll try to get rid of them." Opening the door, I was practically knocked over by the king's men, eager to arrest my guests. "Spies, you say? Is that who they were? They were here but they've gone. They left by the city gate just minutes ago. Quick! Follow them! You might catch them!"

As suddenly as the king's men had entered my house they were gone, shouting, pushing their way through the crowd that had gathered outside my door. Leaping onto their horses, they rode off at full gallop down the road that leads to the fords of the Jordan. Closing the door, I went up to the spies who anxiously awaited me, not knowing until this moment whether I would prove to be their friend or enemy.

"Stay here tonight," I told them. "And then leave through my window on the wall before dawn."

"How can we be sure you won't betray us?" they asked.

"Haven't I just shown you, at great risk to my own life? I have just lied for you and made myself a traitor to my king. What further proof do you need? I know that Yahweh has given you this land. There is no one who hasn't heard of how he dried up the Red Sea for you to leave Egypt, or how he gave you victory over Sihon and Og. The whole land is terrified of you. I no longer have any doubts that Yahweh is God in heaven above and earth below."

"What can we do for you in exchange for our lives?" they asked.

"Spare my life and the lives of my mother and father, brothers and sisters, and their families when Yahweh gives you this city."

"Our lives for yours," they promised me. "If you treat us with kindness, we will treat you and your family with kindness."

Just before dawn, I awakened the two young men. Securing a rope at the window, they let themselves down, dropping the last few feet to the ground. "Go to the hills," I urged them in a whisper. "Your pursuers have gone the other direction. Go to the hills west of here. Wait there three days and then go your way."

"You have our word, we will not harm your family," they assured me, "but only if you mark this house by hanging a scarlet rope out the window."

I did as they said. Within weeks, all that I expected happened, and more. I gathered my family into my home, some came readily, some only after my urgent pleading. For seven days, we waited in silence, door barred, anticipating the assault. When it came, even though I had expected an Israelite victory, I never expected that it would be so swift. Usually the siege of a walled city lasted for years until the besieger gave up and withdrew or until the inhabitants starved. But not this time. At the sound of massed trumpets and the deafening shout of thousands of Israelites, great sections of our city wall collapsed, practically everything except the portion of the wall where my house and family were.

When the din of battle subsided, there was yet another knock at my door. It was the same spies whom I had protected. They brought me and my whole family out, letting us pass through the whole Israelite army in safety. The destruction all around us was horrible to see. All was death and destruction and burning, all but my house. I gave praise to Yahweh.

And Yahweh gave me a husband, Salmon, one of those young spies. I don't know what he saw in me, a fat, fading prostitute. But he seemed delighted to have me, as was my father to have a new son-in-law and a daughter with a reputable occupation, a wife and mother in Israel. Yahweh blessed our union. We had a son, the greatest reward of any woman. We named him Boaz, one day to become the husband of Ruth, the Moabite widow who would become another great-grandmother of Jesus.

Are you surprised at my story, perhaps even disgusted? Don't be. You see, my story is not really about being a prostitute, a liar, and a traitor. It's about grace. It's about how God can take the most unappealing, immoral person and transform that person into his own child, forgiven, washed, made new. It's about how God can bring totally unexpected blessings out of the ashes of sin. He did it for me. Open the door when he knocks, as I did for the spies, and he'll do it for you.

Oh, I told you I was a grandmother, didn't I? Thanks to Matthew, so many of my grandchildren are listed there for you. Let me tell you about them! I just happened to bring pictures.

Prayer

God of all grace, your redemptive power rescued Rahab, a woman of the street, and so renewed her heart that she and her whole family were spared your wrath by faith. Give me such faith and obedience that I, too, might be worthy to be included in that family of the redeemed, the family that calls Rahab Grandmother, and Jesus Brother and Savior. In his name I pray. Amen.

Advent 2 — Children's Sermon

"The men said to (Rahab), 'This oath you made us swear will not be binding on us unless, when we enter the land, you have tied this scarlet cord in the window through which you let us down, and unless you have brought all your family into your house.'"
— Joshua 2:17-18

Items needed: pieces of red rope or yarn to give children

Hello, children! Christmas is getting closer and I'm getting more and more excited. Are you? Tonight we remember Rahab, one of the grandmothers of Jesus. Before she trusted in the Lord, she would break God's laws for money. She knew in her heart that this was wrong. When Rahab turned to God, he forgave her. She became willing to do anything she could to serve him.

Do you know what good she did? *(Let one or two children answer.)* Yes, she hid two of God's people, two spies who would have been killed by the king of Jericho if he knew where they were. The spies were so thankful to Rahab for saving their lives, they asked how they could help her. She told them she believed in the Lord their God and she asked them to spare her family when Israel captured her city.

The spies promised Rahab they would see that she was protected. They told her to gather her whole family into her house and hang a red rope out the window. When the Israelite soldiers saw the red rope, they would not harm anyone in that house. So that's just what Rahab did. And just as the spies had promised, when the attack on Jericho came, Rahab's family was saved.

I've brought a piece of red yarn for each of you to remind you of how God protected Rahab and her family. *(Pass out the pieces of yarn.)* But the yarn also reminds us of something else. What else is red? *(Let several children speak.)* Yes, all of those things are red. The blood of Jesus is red, too. Jesus, whose birth we will celebrate very soon, was born in order that he might grow up and die on the cross to pay for our sins. His blood is like the red rope of Rahab. Just as the red rope saved Rahab and her family, the red blood of Jesus saves everyone who believes in him.

That means that God forgives us of all our sins, gives us the church as our new family, and someday gives us a new home in heaven. That's what God did for Rahab. As God's forgiven child, she married, had children, and even became a grandmother of Jesus. What a wonderful gift God gave her! He gives us wonderful gifts in Jesus, too. Let's thank him.

Prayer

Dear God, thank you for the blood of Jesus that saves me from my sins. Because of Jesus, I am your child and have a wonderful church family and a home in heaven. As Rahab helped the spies, show me how I can help your people, too. In Jesus' name I pray. Amen.

Worship Bulletin

Bethlehem's Closet — A Reunion Of Grace
Meditations For Advent From The Family of Jesus

We Approach Our Gracious God

Hymn "Let The Earth Now Praise The Lord" (vv. 1-4)

Invocation
P: In the name of the Father and of the Son and of the Holy Spirit,
C: **Amen.**

Psalm 105 (Selected verses)
P: Give thanks to the Lord, call on his name; make known among the nations what he has done.
C: **Remember the wonders he has done, his miracles and the judgments he pronounced.**
P: He remembers his covenant forever, the word he commanded for a thousand generations.
C: **The covenant he made with Abraham, the oath he swore to Isaac.**
P: He brought his people out with rejoicing, his chosen ones with shouts of joy;
C: **that they might keep his precepts and observe his laws.**
All: **Praise the Lord!**

Hymn "Let The Earth Now Praise The Lord" (vv. 5-7)

We Hear God's Gracious Word

The First Lesson Joshua 2:1-15
"The Lord your God is God in heaven above and on earth below."

L: This is the record of the family of Jesus.
C: **As Rahab, I am a sinner in need of God's grace.**

The Holy Gospel Matthew 1:1-5a
"Salmon was the father of Boaz whose mother was Rahab."

P: It was for the salvation of this family that Jesus was born.
C: **I am his family. He will save his people from their sins.**

Children's Sermon

Hymn "What Child Is This?"

Sermon "Grandmother Rahab — A Former Prostitute"

We Respond In Faith To God's Gracious Word

The Apostles' Creed
I believe in God the Father Almighty, maker of heaven and earth.
    And in Jesus Christ, his only Son, our Lord, who was conceived by the Holy Spirit, born of the virgin Mary, suffered under Pontius Pilate, was crucified, died and was buried. He descended into hell. The third day he rose again from the dead. He ascended into heaven, and sits at the right hand of God the Father Almighty. From thence he will come to judge the living and the dead.
    I believe in the Holy Spirit, the holy Christian Church, the communion of saints, the forgiveness of sins, the resurrection of the body, and the life everlasting. Amen.

Offering

Offering Voluntary

Prayer Of The Day (Unison)
God of all grace, your redemptive power rescued a woman of the street and so renewed her heart that she and her whole family were spared your wrath by faith. Give me such faith and obedience that I, too, might be worthy to be included in that family of the redeemed, the family that calls Rahab Grandmother, and Jesus Brother and Savior. In his name. Amen.

Pastoral Prayers

Response
P: Grandson of Rahab, Savior,
C: **hear our prayer.**

The Lord's Prayer (Unison)
    Our Father, who art in heaven, hallowed be thy name, thy kingdom come, thy will be done on earth as it is in heaven.
    Give us this day our daily bread; and forgive us our trespasses as we forgive those who trespass against us; and lead us not into temptation, but deliver us from evil.
    For thine is the kingdom and the power and the glory forever and ever. Amen.

We Go Forth To Live God's Gracious Word

Concluding Sentences And Benediction
P: Jesus, Grandson of Rahab, is our Brother.
C: **Yes, Grandson of Rahab, our Brother, yet more than a brother, also the Son of God, our Savior.**
P: Grow in the grace and knowledge of our Lord and Savior Jesus Christ, to him be the glory both now and forever. Amen.

Closing Hymn   "Hark The Glad Sound"

Advent 3   Ruth 1:1—4:22
                                      Matthew 1:1-5 (6)

Grandmother Ruth — A Moabite Convert

Hello, my name is Ruth. May I join you? Mostly men here, I see, except for a few familiar women. Over there, I see Tamar, and next to her, Rahab. At least I won't be the only woman in the place. But I am family, you know, and as family of Jesus, a grandmother in fact, I do belong here, especially since this Bethlehem reunion in honor of Jesus' birthday is a gathering of grace.

I've certainly received my share of grace in abundance. No, I never played prostitute as did my friends Tamar and Rahab, whom you've met. But even so, my ancestry and actions have been criticized by many, especially by King David's enemies.

Some claimed David was unworthy to assume the throne of Israel, especially since I, his great-grandmother, was a Moabite, a non-Jew. My nation descended from Lot, the nephew of Abraham. That's a story in itself. One of Lot's daughters committed incest with him. My ancestor Moab was the result of that union.

So we were cousins of Abraham, but never really accepted as family. As the centuries went by, Israel and Moab generally got along well enough. After all, we had the same language, the same culture, even the same alphabet. The only difference was our religion. We worshiped Chemosh, that angry god whose wrath we would try to appease by sacrificing to him our children. That offended our Israelite cousins, as did our refusal to allow them use of the king's highway to pass through our land on their way to conquer Canaan. Once our king attempted to have Israel cursed by the false prophet, Balaam. He ended up blessing them instead.

The women of my land were famous for being especially beautiful and tempting. We lured many young Israelite men into our tents, and beds, and from there into our religion. The strength of Israel's army was so threatened by us that their leaders put to death their own men and our women whenever they were found together.

So you can see why some would question David's fitness to be king when he came from stock like ours. My story is preserved to show that not all Moabites were the same. Some were people of true faith and virtue, as I have often been described. But if faith and virtue describe me, what, you might ask, was I doing that night long ago, under the blanket with Boaz the Israelite, a man to whom I wasn't married?

Maybe I should go back to the beginning. I had met Mahlon, my first husband, after he came from Bethlehem in Judah with his parents Elimelech and Naomi, and his brother Kilion. They'd been forced off their farm by drought and famine. Things were not as bad in Moab, so they settled among my people. We were so young when we met, Mahlon and I. It was love at first sight. No one was particularly pleased; my family wanted me to marry within my own clan and religion, as did Mahlon's. He wasn't even in good health. His name means "sickly." But we believed love conquers all, so we married. But love didn't conquer all. Within ten years, we'd had more grief than I would have ever thought I could stand. There was famine in Moab too, and along with it disease. First, my father-in-law Elimelech died, then Kilion, my brother-in-law, and finally my husband Mahlon. I was left with nothing except Naomi, and her faith in Yahweh that I now shared.

You can't imagine what it's like to place all your hopes for happiness and a secure future in your husband and children only to be left with neither in a harsh and violent land. It was an even greater tragedy for Naomi. All the men in her family were dead. And there were no grandchildren. Besides that, she was far from home and any relatives who survived. It was the worst possible fate to befall an old woman.

It was better for me. I was still young and attractive. I could have remarried in Moab. But by now that was unthinkable for me. My family worshiped a god who demanded the blood of children. I had given my life to the God of heaven and earth, Yahweh, a God who loved the widow and orphan, the poor and the foreigner. Yahweh loved Naomi, and had chosen to show his love for her through me. It fell upon me to be her friend, fulfilling the meaning of my name, Ruth.

For some, the obligations of friendship, of family, even of religion apply only when the object of one's affections is alive. Most would feel that I was free of all these obligations as they related to Naomi from the moment of my husband's death. They don't understand that mine was not a love and faith that was required by social convention, but rather a love and faith from the heart, that would go with me to the grave. Thus when Naomi urged me to go back to my family, I couldn't.

So I told her, "Where you go I will go, and where you stay I will stay. Your people will be my people and your God my God. Where you die, I will die, and there I will be buried." For my sister-in-law, Orpah, the affection for Naomi remained, but not the obligation. She chose to stay in Moab. I couldn't. I belonged to the God of Israel now, and to his people, and to Naomi's family.

So together we returned to Bethlehem and the long-abandoned farm she still owned. There was shock when the people who had once known Naomi saw her again. Once a beautiful, proud woman with a husband and two sons, now she was an old, stooped widow, poor and alone except for a Moabite daughter-in-law. So deep was her pain she changed her name from Naomi, meaning "pleasant," to Mara, "bitterness."

But we couldn't have returned home at a more hopeful time. The barley harvest was just beginning and soon after that the wheat harvest. For two months I would be able to glean in the fields behind the harvesters, gathering whatever others missed, accumulating the food two widows would need for survival during the coming winter.

Was it accident, or was it divine plan that led me to the field of Boaz to glean? News travels fast in a small town like Bethlehem. Any newcomer is known instantly to everyone. Before I even arrived at Boaz's field, his male and female servants knew all about me. I was the talk of every field hand, but I ignored them all, keeping to myself.

All day long I labored, gathering all I could behind the harvesters. The men would cut the barley stalks with their sickles. The women would follow, gathering them up, tying them into bundles and then laying them in ox and donkey carts. Yahweh had graciously provided for the poor and foreigner in his land by forbidding farmers from harvesting the corners of their fields or gathering what the harvesters dropped. That was for the needy. That is what I was gathering.

That evening, Boaz stopped by to see how the harvest was going. Blessing his workers in the name of Yahweh, he noticed me, asking the others about me. They explained that I was Naomi's widowed daughter-in-law, that I had worked all day in the sun except for a short rest in a shelter. Boaz gazed in my direction a long time, then talked with his workers in low tones that I couldn't make out.

Coming over to me, he introduced himself as Boaz, looking as strong as his name implied. He urged me to work only in his field because I might be in danger somewhere else. He told me I could have all the food and drink I wanted. I didn't understand. "Why would you treat me, a foreigner, with such kindness?" I asked, bowing humbly.

"All you have done for Naomi has been told about you, how you left your father and mother and homeland to care for her, to live among a people you had not known. All this is being spoken of," replied Boaz. "May you be richly rewarded by Yahweh, God of Israel, under whose wings you have come to take refuge."

The kindness of Boaz overwhelmed me. At mealtime, he invited me to eat with him, sharing his bread and wine vinegar. As I left, he had his servants purposefully scatter grain stalks in front of me that I might have plenty to take home to Naomi.

Surprise! Disbelief! Joy! All these were words that described Naomi as she greeted me from the door of the dilapidated homestead. Eyes wide at the huge burden of grain I bore, she cried out, "Where did you glean today? Where did you work? Blessed be the man who took notice of you!"

"His name was Boaz," I answered.

"Boaz? Boaz?" she asked in amazement. "Did you say, 'Boaz'? He's our close relative, a kinsman-redeemer. Indeed, God has not stopped showing his kindness to the living and the dead!" The bitterness fled from Naomi's face, replaced by the pleasantness that fit her so much better.

Day after day, I returned to Boaz's fields. And each day Boaz treated me with the same generosity and kindness. Toward late May, as the harvest was ending, Naomi spoke to me about my future. She had a plan, one that a Moabite woman could be expected to carry out well.

"Boaz is our kinsman," she said. "Tonight, after winnowing at the threshing floor, go to him where he sleeps near his grain, protecting it. Wash. Perfume yourself. Put on your most beautiful clothes. When he is finished eating and drinking, he will lie down. After he is asleep, lift up the blanket and lie at his feet, covering yourself with his garment."

This means more in Hebrew than it does in English. I wasn't being asked to be a foot warmer for Boaz on a cool spring night. I was being asked to expose him in an intimate way. That may sound shocking and forward to you, as though I were being asked to seduce Boaz. In a manner of speaking, I suppose that's exactly what I was being asked to do.

But this was to be no mere midnight rendezvous on the threshing floor. This was a marriage proposal. It was more than that. It was a call to Boaz to do his duty as a kinsman-redeemer, to marry me and raise up children for my deceased husband Mahlon and grandchildren for Naomi. It was the law. And unless Naomi and I had misread all the gestures Boaz had made toward me, marriage is what Boaz wanted too.

He didn't disappoint me. When he awoke in the middle of the night and discovered me in bed with him, I bluntly told him, "As you have prayed that Yahweh would spread his wings over me, may you now be God's answer to that prayer by spreading your wings over me."

Boaz had no trouble understanding what I meant. He asked God's blessings on me for seeking out him as a husband and not a younger man. But then he gave me some distressing information. Though he was in fact a kinsman-redeemer, obligated to protect Naomi and her property, and me as widow of Naomi's son, there was a closer relative. That relative would have to be approached first. "If he will not do it, I will," promised Boaz.

Before dawn, loaded down with six more measures of barley as token of his sincerity, I left Boaz and returned to Naomi, telling her everything that had happened. I didn't know whether to be excited or afraid. Must I marry someone I didn't love or even know? Or would I be able to marry Boaz who had demonstrated over and over his care for me?

"Don't worry, Ruth," Naomi assured me. "Boaz is a man of honor and substance. He will not rest till he sees that whatever is right is done."

And he did. The very next day, Boaz went to the city gate where all the important business deals were concluded and cases of law were settled. Taking his seat with the elders, he waited till our other kinsman-redeemer appeared. After inviting him to take a seat, Boaz addressed him in front of all the elders. I have to admit that his approach was a clever one, speaking first only of the land involved, and then of me.

"Naomi has come back from Moab and is selling the piece of land that belonged to our brother Elimelech. Will you redeem it to keep it in the family and to keep Naomi out of poverty?"

"Of course, I'll redeem it," he answered. "I can always use more land."

"On the day you buy it," Boaz went on, "you also acquire the widow of Naomi's son Mahlon, in whose name you'll own the property and for whom you will raise up children to ensure that his name is carried on."

The kinsman-redeemer coughed, and to my delight said, "Then I can't do it. I would endanger my own estate. You redeem it." Taking off his sandal, he gave it to Boaz, demonstrating for all that he was giving up any claim to the land, as well as me.

I couldn't have been happier as Boaz addressed the elders. He left nothing to doubt, no loose ends. "Today you are witnesses that I have bought from Naomi all the property of Elimelech, Kilion, and Mahlon. I have also acquired Ruth, the Moabitess, Mahlon's widow, as my wife. You are my witnesses."

The whole town of Bethlehem rejoiced with me and Boaz and Naomi, giving us our blessing. And my how we were blessed. The women of Bethlehem honored me by telling Naomi I was better to her than ten sons. How proud I was on the day I was able to place in the arms of Naomi a son born to Boaz and me, Obed, grandfather of David, and one day of Christ.

And it all began in a barley field. You know, once I didn't even like barley, but I've gotten used to it. I wonder if you'd like one of my recipes? It's amazing the things you can stir up with a little barley!

Prayer

Lord, Ruth is a picture of me, your child not because of birth but because of new birth, by faith in your promises, faith you gave me. As a gift, I have become a member of your family, beloved, cared for. May there always be room in my heart for Jesus, as Boaz found room in his heart for Ruth who trusted you. In Jesus' name I pray. Amen.

Advent 3 — Children's Sermon

"I know that my Redeemer lives, and that in the end he will stand upon the earth. And after my skin has been destroyed, yet in my flesh I will see God." — Job 19:25-26

Items needed: barley in zip lock bags

Hi, boys and girls. I imagine some of the Bible stories you've been hearing during our Advent services are new to you. How many of you have ever heard the story of Ruth? *(Count hands.)* A few, good! How many of you have ever heard of a kinsman-redeemer? *(Again, count hands.)* Practically no one. Just as I thought.

The kinsman-redeemer was very important in Bible times. He was a person God used to help poor widows who were all alone. The closest man relative was supposed to pay the poor widow's debts, take care of her land for her, and even marry her so she could have children to provide for her in her old age.

Relatives still take care of lonely or elderly family members. But now there are other ways to help them. There are government programs such as Social Security and food stamps and low-income housing, as well as private charities. But even so, God still wants his people to care for those in need.

I brought some barley with me for each of you. *(Pass out barley bags.)* Besides the protection of a kinsman-redeemer, God's Old Testament people were to let the poor and homeless gather the leftover grain in the fields during and after the harvest. The farmer was not allowed to pick it up or even harvest the corners of his fields. That grain was for the poor people. Wasn't God wonderful to provide for the needy that way?

Today, we still need the same things God's people needed a long time ago. We need someone to keep us safe and rescue us when we're in danger. We need bread for food.

God sent his Son, Jesus, to do all those things for us in a spiritual way. He's like our kinsman-redeemer. The Bible even calls him "Redeemer." Through Jesus' death on the cross, God rescues us from sin, death, and the devil. He forgives us and gives us eternal life. Through his word and sacraments, Jesus feeds us with the special food, giving us faith and strengthening our faith. Let's say, "Thank you," to Jesus.

Prayer

Dear Jesus, thank you for being my Redeemer, for saving me from my enemies, and for giving me a safe home with you forever. Thank you for the Bible, for Holy Baptism and the Lord's Supper which help me trust you. In Jesus' name I pray. Amen.

Worship Bulletin

Bethlehem's Closet — A Reunion Of Grace
Meditations For Advent From The Family of Jesus

We Approach Our Gracious God

Hymn "Lift Up Your Heads, You Mighty Gates" (vv. 1-3)

Invocation
P: In the name of the Father and of the Son and of the Holy Spirit,
C: Amen.

Psalm 50 (Selected verses)
P: The Mighty One, God the Lord, speaks and summons the earth from the rising of the sun to the place where it sets.
C: From Zion, perfect in beauty, God shines forth.
P: He summons the heavens above, and the earth, that he may judge his people.
C: Sacrifice thank offerings to God, fulfill your vows to the Most High,
All: call upon me in the day of trouble; I will deliver you, and you will honor me.

Hymn "Lift Up Your Heads, You Mighty Gates" (vv. 4-5)

We Hear God's Gracious Word

The First Lesson Ruth 1:1-17
"Your people will be my people and your God, my God."

L: This is the record of the family of Jesus,
C: As Ruth, I have no family, apart from God's grace.

The Holy Gospel Matthew 1:1-5a
"Boaz [was] the father of Obed, whose mother was Ruth."

P: It was for the salvation of this family that Jesus was born.
C: I am his family. He will save his people from their sins.

Children's Sermon

Hymn "Gentle Mary Laid Her Child"

Sermon "Grandmother Ruth — A Moabite Convert"

We Respond In Faith To God's Gracious Word

The Apostles' Creed
I believe in God the Father Almighty, maker of heaven and earth.

And in Jesus Christ, his only Son, our Lord, who was conceived by the Holy Spirit, born of the virgin Mary, suffered under Pontius Pilate, was crucified, died and was buried. He descended into hell. The third day he rose again from the dead. He ascended into heaven, and sits at the right hand of God the Father Almighty. From thence he will come to judge the living and the dead.

I believe in the Holy Spirit, the holy Christian Church, the communion of saints, the forgiveness of sins, the resurrection of the body, and the life everlasting. Amen.

Offering

Offering Voluntary

Prayer Of The Day (Unison)
Ruth is a picture of me, your child not because of birth, but because of new birth. By faith in your promises, faith you gave me as a gift, I have become a member of your family, beloved,

cared for. May there always be room in my heart for Jesus, as Boaz found room in his heart for Ruth who trusted you. In Jesus' name. Amen.

Pastoral Prayers

Response
P: Grandson of Ruth, Savior,
C: hear our prayer.

The Lord's Prayer (Unison)
Our Father, who art in heaven, hallowed be thy name, thy kingdom come, thy will be done on earth as it is in heaven. Give us this day our daily bread; and forgive us our trespasses as we forgive those who trespass against us; and lead us not into temptation, but deliver us from evil. For thine is the kingdom and the power and the glory forever and ever. Amen.

We Go Forth To Live God's Gracious Word

Concluding Sentences And Benediction
P: Jesus, Grandson of Ruth, is our Brother.
C: **Yes, Grandson of Ruth, our Brother, yet more than a brother, also the Son of God, our Savior.**
P: May the God who gives endurance and encouragement give you a spirit of unity among yourselves as you follow Christ Jesus so that with one heart and mouth you may glorify the God and Father of our Lord Jesus Christ. Amen.

Closing Hymn   "Come, O Long-Expected Jesus"
(Tune: HYFRYDOL)

Christmas Eve Matthew 1:(1-11) 12-17; Luke 1:26-38; 2:1-20
Isaiah 7:14; 9:1-7; Galatians 4:1-7

Mary — A Young Mother

Oh, you're here! Do come in. I was beginning to worry. Mothers do that, you know. Just about everyone is already here. Oh, there's no need to wipe off your sandals. The floor is made of dirt anyway. It's the best I can afford. As a matter of fact, after my husband Joseph died, I wasn't able to afford anything at all. John, a family friend, took me in.

You don't recognize me? I guess we haven't met, have we? You were expecting a lovely young lady in a white robe and blue veil, not a wrinkled fifty-something widow in this brown homespun. I'm Mary, mother of Jesus. And, yes, this is the reunion of the family of Jesus. I know we aren't actually related, you and I, but if you're a follower of my son, I consider you family, just as though you were my own children. That's why you got the invitation to the reunion. Yes, it's crowded, but there's a seat for you somewhere in here.

I hope you'll get a chance to meet some of Jesus' grandmothers: Tamar, Rahab, and Ruth. Bathsheba is still on her way. I'm sure you'll have so much in common with them. I know I do. You look surprised? I, Mary, have something in common with them, women who include foreigners, adulteresses, and prostitutes? Of course I do. You see, we share a common relative, my son Jesus, and through him, God's grace in abundance.

So much has been written about me, and frankly much of it is legend. One day I was paging through some old books that described a woman who was second only to God. There were pictures of her, looking like a queen, larger than life, cradling a small man in her arms. There were even prayers that replaced God's name with hers. How amazed I was to discover that the woman's name was Mary! I didn't know whether to be amused or angry. I'm sure it was only respect for my role in the redemption story that was intended. But there was little similarity between that Mary and the woman I knew myself to be.

You know, I really had very little to do with what happened to me so long ago. I was just a teenage girl. My parents, Joachim and Ann, had arranged my marriage to Joseph, the carpenter in Nazareth. And no, he wasn't a frail old man, like some of those pictures make him out to be. He was young and strong with black curly hair and a sun-browned face. His hands were rough from the wood he crafted into useful items for home and farm.

My friends were envious that I would marry such a man. Like any girls we talked about the men in our village; who was handsome, who was not; who was engaged, who was available. We listened to the older women gossip about who was pregnant and who was barren. Perhaps the only thing worse than not being able to have a child was to have one out of wedlock, or to be accused by one's husband of not being a virgin on the wedding night.

According to our rabbi, if the husband claimed his wife was not a virgin, but she or her family could prove otherwise, he would have to pay a fine for lying. If the charges could be proven true, the woman would be taken to the door of her father's house where the men of the village would stone her to death. Even if she'd been raped, that was the punishment, because a good girl would have screamed when it happened. To keep quiet was the same thing as admitting guilt. There was nothing but shame and fear of death for a pregnant woman without a husband. And that's just the situation I found myself in.

My girlhood faith was no greater or less than any other girl's in Nazareth. My father, Joachim, was the religious leader in my home. As a Jewish man, he along with the other men in town conducted the affairs of the synagogue, seeing to it that the law of God was taught and the boys went to school.

It wasn't considered necessary for girls to learn to read and write and study the Torah. We were taught the skills of motherhood and homemaking. But even so, my mother, Ann, told me the stories of godly women of the past: Deborah, warrior, judge and mother in Israel, and Hannah, wife of Elkanah, mother of the prophet

Samuel. Little did I know that someday my song of God's grace and power would be so much like theirs.

Then it happened. With my wedding to Joseph still months away, I received news that would change my life, and indeed the whole world. I was visited by an angel, yes, the Archangel Gabriel no less! I had heard the stories of angels, the cherubim who with flaming swords drove Adam and Eve from the Garden of Eden, the six-winged seraphim in Isaiah's vision who surrounded the throne of God, crying out, "Holy, holy, holy is the LORD, God of Hosts," and even Gabriel who revealed to Daniel the terrifying events of the last days. And now this same Gabriel was visiting me.

Just think, he who had been in the very presence of God and who shone with the brightness of heaven, he who had the power to wage war against the demons of hell and change the course of history at God's command, this very Gabriel appeared to me!

And he told me, "Greetings, you who are highly favored! The Lord is with you." The brilliance of the light that radiated from him drove me to my knees. I was shaking violently, unable to speak. "Don't be afraid," he said. By now it was rather like telling a wet baby not to cry.

I was afraid. But he continued speaking anyway, hardly giving me an opportunity to recover. "You will be with child and give birth to a son, and you are to give him the name Jesus. He will be great and will be called the Son of the Most High. The Lord God will give him the throne of his father David, and he will reign over the house of Jacob forever; his kingdom will never end."

Who this child would be at that moment seemed less important to me than how I would conceive him. Pregnancy outside of wedlock could mean my death. "How will this be, since I am a virgin?" I managed to ask him.

The angel's reply raised more questions than it gave answers. "The Holy Spirit will come upon you, and the power of the Most High will overshadow you. So the Holy One to be born will be called the Son of God." I didn't know what that meant except that somehow God's power would enable me to conceive. No man, not even Joseph my betrothed, himself a descendant of kings, would be involved.

Again the angel Gabriel spoke, "For nothing will be impossible with God." I believed, though I didn't understand. And it is for this reason, faith that accepted God's will and promise, faith that enabled me to submit to God's will for my life, that I was to be called "blessed" by Christians ever since.

If you were to look at other events in my life, you might doubt my faith. There's the time I was worried about my son's mental health. He'd been preaching and healing day after day without rest. Yes, he was God's Son, but he was my son too, a human being like all of us. And as his mother I was concerned about him. I came to take him home, fearing he'd had a nervous breakdown. You'd allow me a mother's right to worry, wouldn't you?

But he didn't. With a great sweep of his arm toward the crowd that had gathered, that great multitude of the untaught and the sick, he said, "These are my mother and brothers and sisters." It forced me to realize that his mission was not just to fulfill the needs and longings of his mother, but to do the work of his Father, a task that would consume his very life.

God couldn't have provided me with a better husband for the role I'd been given as mother of God's Son. Earlier I told you what a strong young man Joseph was. Those pictures you've seen of him as being old and gray were designed to make you think he must have had no desire for me as a woman. That way he would keep me a virgin, a fit vessel to bear God's Son. But that's not the way it was.

Joseph and I, as a young couple with all the normal desires of youth, had yearned for the day we could be intimate. Part of the beauty of our story is that Joseph also believed and surrendered his will to God's. Without argument, without resentment, Joseph denied himself so that the son whom he would adopt would be born of his virgin wife. If there is a true saint in this story, it is Joseph, my husband.

He made certain that I would suffer no shame in my pregnancy. Partly to prevent tongues from wagging in Nazareth, and partly that my own faith might be reinforced, Joseph sent me to visit my elderly aunt, Elizabeth. There I saw for myself that miracles such as mine could truly happen. She and Zechariah, both well past the age of childbearing, were to have a son also. His name would be John, cousin of Jesus. One day as John the Baptizer, he would proclaim my son to be "the Lamb of God who takes away the sins of the world."

From the hill country of Judah where Elizabeth and Zechariah lived, Joseph and I continued on to Bethlehem, the ancestral home of his family. Caesar had decreed that a census be taken for purposes of taxation and that all subject peoples return to their places of origin. At the time we didn't realize that doing so would also fulfill the ancient prophecy that a descendant of David, an heir to his throne, would be born in Bethlehem. Joseph was of the royal line of David. By birth in Bethlehem into the family of Joseph, and at God's decree, my son would be King.

I was awed, amazed, filled with wonder that I should be the mother of Jesus, the Son of God, the son of David. As the years passed, the outward circumstances might cause one to question that. My son, after learning the carpenter's trade, grew up and left home, becoming a preacher and worker of miracles. I remained an obscure housewife in Nazareth. Occasionally, when Jesus was near home, I would join him at one of the outdoor meetings or at a celebration such as a friend's wedding. He did his first miracle at my request, turning water to wine at Cana.

At first I was thrilled with his popularity, the admiration that people had for him. But it didn't last. His constant challenging of the hypocrisy of the religious leaders earned him their hatred. The crowds became smaller and many turned against him. There were threats against his life. With every threat and insult, as his mother I worried. When the ugliness came to a head — betrayal by Judas, the trials, the torture, the crucifixion — I felt his agony as only a mother can.

At the cross I learned that though he was the Son of God, he was still my son. Those moments when he had seemed indifferent to me were not signs of rejection, but signs of a greater mission. Now at the cross, he fulfilled that mission, dying for sinners, for his ancestors, for you, for me. But he did even more on that gloomiest of days. He remembered me, his mother, a widow, an old woman alone. He said to me and his friend John as we stood together near the cross, "Woman, behold your son," and then to him, "Behold, your mother." From that day, John took me into his home and cared for me as if he were my own son.

    And I suppose in a way he was. Because I gave birth to Jesus who calls sinners he died to save "brother" and "sister," then I must be their mother, and your mother too, in a manner of speaking. So if you'd like to call me Mother Mary, I don't mind.

    Now if you'll excuse me, there's a reunion going on, a celebration of grace. I do hope there's enough wine. I'd hate to embarrass Jesus with another such request at his own party. Come. Let's celebrate together!

Prayer

    Lord God, even as your servant Mary innocently endured humiliation when she was pregnant with Jesus, our Savior and your Son, help me also to be willing to suffer all and pay any price to do your will. In the name of Jesus I pray. Amen.

Christmas Eve — Children's Sermon

"In the sixth month, God sent the angel Gabriel to Nazareth, a town in Galilee, to a virgin pledged to be married to a man named Joseph, a descendant of David. The virgin's name was Mary."

— Luke 1:26-27

Items needed: engagement ring or wedding ring, real or toy

Merry Christmas! Say, is anybody afraid of Christmas? Of course not! Almost everyone is happy about Christmas, because it's the day we celebrate Jesus' birthday. But when Mary and Joseph first heard that Jesus would be born, they were more afraid than happy.

See what I brought to show you? *(Show the engagement ring, letting children look at it and try it on.)* What is it? Yes, it's an engagement ring. An engagement ring symbolizes the promises a man and woman make to each other. Can you think of some of those promises? *(Let children suggest some promises.)*

When Mary and Joseph were engaged, they promised that someday they would get married. They promised that there would be no man or woman in their lives but each other. By being engaged, they were letting everyone else know they had made these promises.

Mary was a virgin. That means she had never been with a man before; she had never been intimate. That's just the way God intends it to be for all of us until we get married. He wants us to keep ourselves pure for the person we marry. That's what Mary and Joseph had promised to each other.

But then came some frightening news from an angel. Perhaps that's part of why it was frightening. Angels were bright and big and powerful, and came from God's presence. First the angel came to Mary and told her she would have a child, Jesus the Son of God. Mary wondered how this would be since she was a virgin. The angel told her the power of God would make it happen. Mary was a woman of faith and believed the angel.

When Joseph learned that Mary was pregnant, he thought she must have broken their promise. He planned to marry her and then divorce her quietly to save her from embarrassment. Then the angel told Joseph that the child Mary would bear was from God. It was a miracle! Joseph believed the angel too.

What a wonderful story! Mary becomes the mother of the Son of God and both she and Joseph keep their promises. God keeps his promises to us, too. Are you baptized? *(Most children will say, "Yes.")* Good! That's the sign of God's promise to you that you are his child. As his child, God will do for you everything he promises. God will forgive your sins and give you a home in heaven, all because Mary's child was our Savior who would one day die for our sins.

Prayer

Dear Father, thank you for the miracle of your Son's birth. Help me to know that because Jesus was born and died for me, I am your child and will live with you forever. In Jesus' name I pray. Amen.

Worship Bulletin

Christmas Eve

We Approach Our Gracious God

Hymn "Oh, Come, All Ye Faithful"
Invocation
P: In the name of the Father and of the Son and of the Holy Spirit,
C: **Amen.**

(Lighting of the Advent Wreath)

P: When all was still, and it was midnight, your almighty Word, O Lord, descended from the royal throne. In him was life, and that life was the light of men. The light shines in the darkness, but the darkness has not understood it.

Hymn "A Great And Mighty Wonder" (vv. 1-3)

Luke 1:46-55 "The Magnificat"
P: And Mary said: "My soul glorifies the Lord,
C: **and my spirit rejoices in God my Savior,**
P: for he has been mindful of the humble state of his servant. From now on all generations will call me blessed,
C: **for the Mighty One has done great things for me — holy is his name.**
P: His mercy extends to those who fear him, from generation to generation.
C: **He has performed mighty deeds with his arm; he has scattered those who are proud in their inmost thoughts.**
P: He has brought down rulers from their thrones but has lifted up the humble.
C: **He has filled the hungry with good things but has sent the rich away empty.**

All: He has helped his servant Israel, remembering to be merciful to Abraham and his descendants forever, even as he said to our fathers."

Hymn "A Great And Mighty Wonder" (vv. 4-5)

Confession And Absolution
P: Let us humble ourselves before Almighty God, confessing our sins to him and begging his forgiveness.

(Silent confession)

P: On this holy Christmas Eve, we consider the birth of our Savior and our great need for him. We confess before God and to one another that we are by nature and action sinners in need of forgiveness. God's holy law reveals our many sins against him and one another. Humbly, we bow before Jesus, the sinless Lamb of God, sent to be our Savior, and confess our sins.
C: **Lord Jesus, I could never fulfill God's righteous demands, but you have, for me. Forgive my sins of thought, word, action, and inaction, not because I am worthy, but because you are. In your name I pray. Amen.**
P: Hear the Good News of great joy! For Jesus' sake, God forgives you all your sins in the name of the Father, Son, and Holy Spirit.
C: **Thanks be to God!**

We Hear God's Gracious Word

The First Lesson Isaiah 9:2-7
"The prophet foretells the coming of Christ."

L: The Old Testament Reading for Christmas Eve is from the ninth chapter of Isaiah.

This is the Word of the Lord.
C: Thanks be to God.

The Epistle Lesson Galatians 4:1-7
"Through Mary's child we are no longer slaves, but sons of God."

L: The Epistle is from the fourth chapter of Galatians.
This is the Word of the Lord.
C: Thanks be to God.

Hymn "What Child Is This?"

The Holy Gospel Luke 1:26-38
"In faith, Mary accepts God's will."

P: The Holy Gospel according to Saint Luke, the first chapter.
This is the Gospel of the Lord.
C: Praise to you, O Christ.

Hymn "Angels We Have Heard On High"

Children's Sermon

Hymn "From Heaven Above To Earth I Come"

Sermon "Mary — A Young Mother"

We Respond In Faith To God's Gracious Word

Nicene Creed
I believe in one God, the Father Almighty, maker of heaven and earth and of all things visible and invisible.
   And in one Lord Jesus Christ, the only-begotten Son of God, begotten of his Father before all worlds, God of God, Light of Light, very God of very God, begotten, not made, being of one substance with the Father, by whom all things were made;

who for us men and for our salvation came down from heaven and was incarnate by the Holy Spirit of the virgin Mary and was made man; and was crucified also for us under Pontius Pilate. He suffered and was buried. And the third day he rose again according to the Scriptures and ascended into heaven and sits at the right hand of the Father. And he will come again with glory to judge both the living and the dead, whose kingdom will have no end.

And I believe in the Holy Spirit, the Lord and Giver of Life, who proceeds from the Father and the Son, who with the Father and the Son together is worshiped and glorified, who spoke by the prophets.

And I believe in one Holy Christian and apostolic church, I acknowledge one baptism for the remission of sins, and I look for the resurrection of the dead and the life of the world to come. Amen.

Offering

Offering Hymn (or Voluntary)   "Once In David's Royal City"

Offering Prayer
P: Father in heaven, we believe but do not understand the miracle of the incarnation of Jesus, your Son, in being born to the virgin Mary. As you gave him to us, help us give ourselves and all we have to you, including these offerings. In Jesus' name,
C: **Amen.**

The Prayers

Pastoral Prayers
P: Let us pray for all people according to their needs.

Response
P: Jesus, Son of God, Son of Mary,
C: **hear our prayer.**

The Lord's Prayer (Unison)
   Our Father, who art in heaven, hallowed be thy name, thy kingdom come, thy will be done on earth as it is in heaven.
   Give us this day our daily bread; and forgive us our trespasses as we forgive those who trespass against us; and lead us not into temptation, but deliver us from evil.
   For thine is the kingdom and the power and the glory forever and ever. Amen.

We Receive God's Grace In The Lord's Supper

(The Order for Holy Communion follows local practice.)

Distribution Hymns   "I Am So Glad When Christmas Comes"
                         "Hark! The Herald Angels Sing"

Lighting Of The Candles
(Acolyte lights ushers' candles with flame from the Christ candle. Ushers in turn give light to the worshiper nearest the aisle, who will pass it on to the others in that row. Please tip the UNLIT candle toward the LIT candle to avoid spilling hot wax.)

P: Jesus said: "I am the Light of the world; whoever follows me will never walk in darkness, but will have the Light of life" (John 8:12b).
C: **We are a people belonging to God, that we may declare the praises of him who called us out of darkness into his wonderful light (1 Peter 2:9b, adapted).**

Hymn   "Silent Night"

We Go Forth To Live God's Gracious Word

Concluding Sentences And Benediction
P: Jesus, Son of Mary, is our Brother.

C: **Yes, Son of Mary, our Brother, yet more than a brother, also the Son of God, our Savior.**
P: Do not be afraid, the angel tells the shepherds and us. I bring you good news of great joy that will be for all the people.
C: **Today in the town of David a Savior has been born to us. He is Christ the Lord.**
P: Glory to God in the highest and on earth peace to men on whom his favor rests.
All: **Amen.**

Closing Hymn "Joy To The World"

Christmas Day   2 Samuel 1-2
Psalm 51; Matthew 1:1-17

Grandmother Bathsheba — A Violated Wife

My name is Bathsheba, wife of David the king. May I join you for this reunion of grace? I hesitated to come inside since my name was not listed in the genealogy. But no one else is the former wife of Uriah and mother of David's son Solomon. So, if you don't mind, I'll just sit right here with you at the table.

Frankly, I'm puzzled why Matthew referred to me but didn't mention my name. Surely he, among all the apostles, understood grace. After all he had been an outcast himself, a tax collector working for the Romans before he met my grandson Jesus. Perhaps he accepted Tamar, Rahab, and Ruth and included their names in his genealogy because their relationship to the king was more remote than mine.

David was Israel's greatest and most beloved king. He's even held up in prophetic scripture as the ideal king. It was hoped that the Messiah would be like the David of popular memory. But mentioning my name in the same sentence with David would tarnish that image. Until I came into David's life, one noble story after another had been told of him, stories of his faith, of his exploits.

Most of you remember only that David, when he was a boy, answered the challenge of the Philistine Goliath and killed him with only a stone and sling. You remember how he faithfully served King Saul, even though Saul, out of jealousy, tried again and again to kill him. You remember the beauty of his Psalms, verses that eloquently speak to every condition of the human heart.

But when it comes to my relationship with David, so many of you choose to forget. And I can understand. It was a story of sin and deceit so black that you wonder how any good thing could come from remembering it. Some, trying to vindicate David, blame me for what happened. That's not really fair. What choice did I have?

Besides being a man after God's heart, David was also king after the most ancient oriental tradition. He was an absolute monarch believed by all the people, including prophets and priests, to have gotten his office from God himself. As such, he held the power of life and death over all his subjects, including me.

It was a warm day in spring when those awful events began to unfold. David's palace in Jerusalem stood high above the homes of his subjects, including mine. And that's as it should be for the king's house. Since my husband Uriah was a trusted and faithful army officer, our house was near the palace where he could be immediately summoned by the king.

The army had taken to the field for a campaign against the Ammonites across the Jordan. Their king, a friend of David's, had died. David had sent a delegation to convey his sympathy to the king's son. The son, evil, not like his father, accused the delegation of being spies. He had their beards shaved and their robes cut off, exposing them. David replied to this insult by laying siege to their capital city, Rabbah.

That's where David should have been, there with his army, encouraging, directing, leading the assault. But by the time I met him he was tired of war, and getting soft in his middle age. So he sent Joab, his general, to take the city without him. It was while the army and my husband were gone doing their duty that David saw me bathing on my roof. Had he been where he should have been, it never would have happened.

My house was like others in Jerusalem, having few windows and a flat roof that could be reached by stairs from inside. In the heat of the day, the roof was a good place to dry the wash or maybe the flax that had been harvested. In the evening the roof was so much cooler than the rooms within the house. That's where I, and most people, would bathe and sleep.

I was bathing when David saw me. It was never my intent to attract his attention. His first notice of me was purely accidental. But when his gaze lingered, it moved beyond the accidental to lust. He sent a servant to inquire who I was, coming to my door later that evening. "I am Bathsheba, wife of Uriah the king's trusted soldier, daughter of Eliam, also soldier of the king, and granddaughter of Ahithophel, advisor to the king."

Knowing all this, and that nothing but trouble and disgrace could come from intimacy with me, David sent for me anyway. I had no idea why he wanted me to come and I had no reason to suspect that his intent was evil. Why would the king contemplate an act that would disaffect so many of his most faithful servants? So, I went. And he forced himself on me.

What could I have done? This man who had subdued all his enemies in battle, this man who had personally killed thousands of Philistines, this man whose army at that very moment was subduing one of the last bastions of resistance to his authority, this same man held my life in his hands. To protest would mean death. To tell someone else would invite disbelief. So I submitted.

When it was over I returned home and washed, again and again, trying to purify myself from the uncleaness. How could I face my husband, my father, my grandfather? Though I had done nothing wrong, as even the official record of the events will show, yet I felt guilty before God.

My husband was still on the battlefield with the army when I realized I was pregnant. I had neither seen nor spoken to the king since it happened. But now I had to. When Uriah returned, he would discover that I carried a child that was not his, and though he was a godly man, whose name means "the Light of Yahweh," still he could have me stoned to death, or at the very least he would divorce me in disgrace. Only the king could solve this problem, so I sent word to him, "I am pregnant."

From that moment on, David revealed the great capacity of his heart for wickedness. Perhaps never has there been a man who was such a saint and sinner at the same time. In rapid succession, he broke the commandments of God, one after another. First coveting me, another man's wife. Then stealing me for his adulterous designs. Then trying to cover it up by bringing Uriah home from the war to lie with me. If Uriah had done so, he would have thought the child I carried was his own. But he was a man of honor and devotion to his troops. He refused, twice in fact, even when David, under pretext of friendship, made him drunk.

Failing at false witness, David sent my husband back to the battle carrying a secret message to Joab the commander, ordering him to see that my husband was killed in battle. The order was obeyed. Joab ordered my husband to the wall of the city where he was struck down in a hail of arrows. David hadn't done the deed, but he was responsible. He was the murderer of my husband, just as surely as if the arrow had come from his own bow.

He feigned mourning, and allowed me a brief time to grieve. Then I was summoned once again to the palace where we were married. It almost looked as though David had gotten away with it. But he hadn't. "Be sure your sins will find you out," scripture says, and they did.

Before long, Nathan the prophet made an appearance at the palace. He came to tell David the story of an injustice he'd learned of. A rich man with hundreds of sheep had been visited by a foreign guest. Too greedy to feed his guest with a sheep from his own flock, the rich man stole a sheep, a little ewe lamb from a poor man, the only sheep he owned. "What do you think should be done?" asked Nathan.

David, not realizing Nathan was describing what the king had done, condemned himself, "As surely as Yahweh lives, the man who has done this deserves to die!"

"You are the man," Nathan replied. He knew the whole story of what David had done, reciting it in detail to the king. Then he pronounced God's judgment on David. Violence and the sword would never depart from David's house. Usurpers would try to take his throne. His own son, Absolom, would humiliate the king by lying with the women of his harem in broad daylight. And worse, my baby would die when only seven days old, too young to be circumcised and claimed as God's child and heir of his covenant blessings.

All this would befall David as judgment on his sins. I suffered much, more than I can ever express to you: shame, the death of my husband, the loss of my first child. But never did Nathan the prophet say it was the result of my sin. To be sure, I am a sinner too, but I was not in those events. In those events, I was innocent.

So for you, David may be a hero, the great soldier, slayer of Goliath, singer of Psalms. To me he's a weak sinner who violated me and committed treachery against his friends. Yet he taught me much of the meaning of God's grace. If David is a hero, it is by God's grace through faith. I must say this for David: when confronted by Nathan, he didn't lie. He didn't make excuses. He didn't claim he was ill. He humbly and honestly admitted everything. He said, "I have sinned against the LORD."

David's sin wasn't private. It was a public humiliation of me, my husband, and my family. And because it was public, David confessed his sin publicly. Going to the house of God, which was still a tent in those days, he read before all who were assembled there Psalm 51,which he had written. "Have mercy on me, O God," he begged. "Wash away my iniquity. My sin is always before me. Against you, you only have I sinned. Cleanse me."

Despite the greatness of his sin, God heard his plea and forgave him. The prophet, as God's representative, spoke the comforting words of absolution to him. "The LORD has taken away your sin," Nathan assured him. Nevertheless, the consequences of sin remained, the death of my son, a legacy of violence and intrigue in the family that I became a part of.

Nothing could take away my grief, but in the midst of it God gave me consolation. As the wife of David, I bore another son, Solomon, whom God also loved and whom he named king after David. His name means "peace." To show that God still loved David, and that I too was his beloved child, Solomon would be Israel's most powerful king, a king whose reign would be characterized by peace.

I hope you aren't offended or disillusioned by learning these things about one who is the hero of every Sunday school boy. He can still be your hero if you remember that his heroism is not found in the goodness or purity of his life but in his example of humble repentance and faith. That is what makes any child of God great, including me. It wasn't my innocence that merited reference to me in the genealogy of my grandson Jesus, but grace, grace that covers my sins as well as yours.

Well, there you have it. You know my story, and Tamar's, and Rahab's, and Ruth's, even Mary's. I hope from all our stories you remember one thing, that the real story here is not one of our embarrassments, our humiliations, the indignities we suffered, the brazen sins we committed. That's not the story. The real story is the one that tells of my grandson, Jesus, whose birth we all looked forward to, Jesus, whose name means "The LORD saves."

Without Jesus all our stories would have had unhappy endings. But because he was born and died and rose for me and you, our stories are songs of joy, songs of forgiveness, songs of inclusion in God's family. Because of Jesus' story, no one is left outside. Everyone is invited to the family reunion in Bethlehem, the reunion of grace.

Prayer

Lord, gracious Father, sometimes my guilt is false, as was Bathsheba's. Sometimes my guilt is real, as was David's. Whichever it is, through Jesus, I'm healed, forgiven, and made new. Give me faith to accept your love and grace. Give me humility that invites others to receive your love and grace. I pray in the name of Jesus, son of Mary, grandson of Tamar, Rahab, Ruth, and Bathsheba, Jesus, Son of God and my Savior. Amen.

Christmas Day — Children's Sermon

"One evening David got up from his bed and walked around on the roof of the palace. From the roof he saw a woman bathing. The woman was very beautiful." — 2 Samuel 11:2

Items needed: homemade candy or cookies

I bet every child here knows what today is. What day is it? *(Several children will say "Christmas!")* One of the things I look forward to at Christmas is all the delicious cookies and candy people share with me. Do you have some of those things at home?

Sometimes our grandmas bake goodies and give them to us, cookies like these. *(Give each child a cookie.)* Maybe your grandma is coming to spend Christmas day with you and she'll bring something special to eat. I have many happy memories of all my grandmas. I would sometimes stay with them. They would take me to fun places and cook wonderful meals. Their houses each had a different smell.

In my opinion, my grandmas were all perfect. They loved me and gave me things. If you're a child that's what's important. Cookies at Christmas remind me of my grandmas. It wasn't until I grew up that I found out my grandmothers weren't perfect after all. I learned from my parents and other relatives that some of my grandmas had done bad things. That surprised me and made me very sad. I didn't want to believe it.

That's the way Jesus' grandmas were. I'm sure their grandchildren loved them very much. But when those grandmas were young women, some of them did very bad things. Some had been prostitutes. Some had worshiped idols. Some had told lies. Do you think that made any difference to their grandchildren? No! The grandchildren didn't know those things and loved them anyway.

That's like God's love for us. We've all sinned. We've disobeyed God. But God sent Jesus, through many, many grandmothers, to die for our sins and bring us God's forgiveness. Now God doesn't see all our sins. He only sees the goodness of Jesus when he looks at us.

When you grow up and maybe learn that your grandmother did some really bad things when she was younger, you can forgive her and still think of her as good, even perfect, by faith in Jesus who died for her just as he died for you.

Prayer

Dear God, you have blessed me with grandparents and parents and aunts and uncles who love me and do so many kind things for me. I think they must be perfect. Someday I might learn they aren't as perfect as I think they are now. If that should happen, help me to love them and forgive them for Christ's sake, just as you love me. In Jesus' name I pray. Amen.

Worship Bulletin

Christmas Day

We Approach Our Gracious God

Hymn "Welcome To Earth" (vv. 1-4)

Invocation
P: In the name of the Father and of the Son and of the Holy Spirit,
C: **Amen.**

Confession (Psalm 51)
P: Let us confess our sins to God and ask his forgiveness. Have mercy on me, O God, according to your unfailing love; according to your great compassion blot out my transgressions.
C: **Wash away all my iniquity and cleanse me from my sin.**
P: For I know my transgressions, and my sin is always before me.
C: **Against you, you only, have I sinned and done what is evil in your sight, so that you are proved right when you speak and justified when you judge.**
P: Surely I was sinful at birth, sinful from the time my mother conceived me.
C: **Surely you desire truth in the inner parts; you teach me wisdom in the inmost place.**
P: Cleanse me with hyssop, and I will be clean; wash me, and I will be whiter than snow.
C: **Let me hear joy and gladness; let the bones you have crushed rejoice.**
P: Hide your face from my sins and blot out all my iniquity.
All: **Create in me a pure heart, O God, and renew a steadfast spirit within me.**

(Silence for reflection)

C: Lord, it was to take away the guilt and penalty of my sins that you sent Jesus. I confess my unworthiness, having broken all your laws both outwardly and in my heart. With David, I beg your forgiveness.

P: Hear the Good News! If you confess with your mouth Jesus is Lord and believe in your heart that God raised him from the dead, you will be saved (Romans 10:9). May your hearts be lifted in joy! You are forgiven in the name of the Father and of the Son and of the Holy Spirit.

C: **Amen.**

We Hear God's Gracious Word

The First Lesson 2 Samuel 11:1-27
"The thing David had done displeased the Lord."

P: The Old Testament Lesson is from the eleventh chapter of Second Samuel.
This is the Word of the Lord, sharper than any double-edged sword.

C: **It is this word that judges the thoughts and attitudes of the heart. Thanks be to God.**

The Holy Gospel Matthew 1:1-6
"David was the father of Solomon, whose mother had been Uriah's wife."

P: For the salvation of his family, Jesus was born.

C: **I am his family. He will save his people from their sins.**

Children's Sermon

Hymn "It Came Upon A Midnight Clear"

Sermon "Bathsheba — A Violated Wife"

We Respond In Faith To God's Gracious Word

Nicene Creed
I believe in one God, the Father Almighty, maker of heaven and earth and of all things visible and invisible.

And in one Lord Jesus Christ, the only-begotten Son of God, begotten of his Father before all worlds, God of God, Light of Light, very God of very God, begotten, not made, being of one substance with the Father, by whom all things were made; who for us men and for our salvation came down from heaven and was incarnate by the Holy Spirit of the virgin Mary and was made man; and was crucified also for us under Pontius Pilate. He suffered and was buried. And the third day he rose again according to the Scriptures and ascended into heaven and sits at the right hand of the Father. And he will come again with glory to judge both the living and the dead, whose kingdom will have no end.

And I believe in the Holy Spirit, the Lord and Giver of Life, who proceeds from the Father and the Son, who with the Father and the Son together is worshiped and glorified, who spoke by the prophets.

And I believe in one Holy Christian and apostolic church, I acknowledge one baptism for the remission of sins, and I look for the resurrection of the dead and the life of the world to come. Amen.

Offering

Offering Hymn

Prayer Of The Day (Unison)
Lord Jesus, you humbled yourself to be born not only of a virgin, but also into a family of sinners like Tamar, Rahab, Ruth, Bathsheba, and, yes, me also. As your grace touched all their lives, may it also transform me, and move me to invite and welcome to your family all who will accept your gifts of

forgiveness and eternal life. In your name, you who are one God with the Father and the Holy Spirit. Amen.

Pastoral Prayers
P: Jesus, Son of God, Grandson of Bathsheba,
C: hear our prayer.

The Lord's Prayer (Unison)
Our Father, who art in heaven, hallowed be thy name, thy kingdom come, thy will be done on earth as it is in heaven.
Give us this day our daily bread; and forgive us our trespasses as we forgive those who trespass against us; and lead us not into temptation, but deliver us from evil.
For thine is the kingdom and the power and the glory forever and ever. Amen.

We Receive God's Grace In The Lord's Supper

(The Order for Holy Communion follows local practice.)

Distribution Hymns   "Silent Night"
                              "We Praise, O Christ" (vv. 1-4)

We Go Forth To Live God's Gracious Word

Concluding Sentences And Benediction
P: Jesus, Grandson of Bathsheba, is our Brother.
C: **Yes, Grandson of Bathsheba, our Brother, yet more than a brother, also the Son of God, our Savior.**
P: Sovereign Lord, as you have promised, you now dismiss your servant in peace.
C: **For my eyes have seen your salvation which you have prepared in the sight of all people.**
P: A light of revelation to the Gentiles,
C: **and the glory of your people Israel.**

P: May the God of hope fill you with all joy and peace as you trust in his Son, Jesus Christ, so that you may overflow with hope by the power of the Holy Spirit.
All: **Amen.**

Closing Hymn "Now Sing We, Now Rejoice"